Around the World
with Kate & Mack

A Look at Languages from A to Z

Visit Wycliffe's website at wycliffe.org.

Around the World with Kate & Mack
A Look at Languages from A to Z
© 2014 Wycliffe Bible Translators, Inc.
Written by Melissa Paredes
Illustrations by Ben Rupp
Published by Wycliffe Bible Translators, Inc.

ISBN 978-0-938978-49-7

Printed in the United States of America

First printing 2014 by Wycliffe Bible Translators, Inc.

Around the World
with Kate & Mack

A Look at Languages from A to Z

Written by Melissa Paredes

Illustrated by Ben Rupp

wycliffe.org/A-Z

Wycliffe®

Table of Contents

Kate & Mack

Kate

Mack

Hi, kids! My name is Kate. This is my best friend, Mack. We're going to be your tour guides today!

My parents are missionaries with Wycliffe Bible Translators in Mexico. That's where I was born. It's also where I met Mack.

Mack and I love to learn about the world. We especially like to learn about people and all the languages they speak.

Mexico

Did you know that there are almost seven thousand languages spoken around the world? That's a lot!

My dad says it's important to be able to understand the Bible in your heart language. When I was little, I didn't know what that meant. So I asked him. He said that many people speak more than one language. They might speak the language their parents taught them, and also another language, like English. But their heart language is the one they dream in, think in, and talk to God in. My dad also said that many people still don't have the Bible in their heart language.

Dream Think Pray

That's why my parents work with Wycliffe. They are helping to translate the Bible for people who don't have one yet.

Mack and I wanted to learn more about some of these languages that don't have a Bible, so we traveled to many different countries.

We got to meet a lot of kids and learn what their lives are like. We also got to learn lots of cool facts about different countries and people that we didn't know before. Like, did you know that there are 7,107 islands in the Philippines? And people live on only 2,000 of them!

We have so much we want to show you! To make this easy, we've chosen one language for every letter of the alphabet—all the way from A to Z.

Arop
(AH-rop)

PAPUA NEW GUINEA

Hi! My name is Anna, and I'm going to tell you about Arop, a small village in Papua New Guinea where my mother grew up. Arop used to sit on a thin strip of beach that we call a sand spit, and all the houses were built on stilts. Because my mother lived on the beach, she learned how to use a canoe when she was only three years old! Her father would work in garden, and her mother would make yummy food. Sometimes her brothers would climb coconut trees, and get the fruit to eat and drink the juice inside. Coconuts were her favorite, and now they're my favorite too!

Anna

4.

My mother loved living in Arop. But one day, a big wave came crashing over the village. Then a second wave hit, and a third one! Village houses were swept away by these big waves. Tall coconut trees lay flat on the ground everywhere. But the worst part was that a lot of the people in the village were swept away by the waves. As the survivors gathered together in the days that followed, they realized how many had lost family members. They also realized that they couldn't live there anymore. It was too dangerous! They would have to start a new village, but where?

They decided to move inland where their gardens were, where they were safe from crashing waves. It was hard to adjust to a new place to live. Everyone was very sad to leave their beach home.

My mother remembers that two missionaries helped her family a lot. Their names were John and Bonnie Nystrom, and they had moved to Arop several years before the waves washed away the village. John and Bonnie had come to learn the Arop language, create an alphabet, and help translate the Bible! They taught people to read using the alphabet.

My mother was very excited, and so were many people in the village! Now they could learn to read and write, and share stories about the big waves!

Many years later, I was born. Now I'm eight years old. The Arop people have made their new village a home. They still miss the beach sometimes, but they can tell you stories about what life used to be like. And many people are excited because they've learned to read and write. Most importantly we've learned about Jesus! God has taught us that even when there are big waves in life, He is bigger than the waves, and we can trust in Him for everything.

Bonnie & John
↓

6

FUN FACTS:

shell money

Kina

- 🌐 Papua New Guinea is one of the very few places on earth that is close to the equator but still has snow in very high altitudes!

- 🌐 There are over 800 different languages in this country! Papua New Guinea is also one of the three countries with the greatest need for Bible translation—in the whole world!

- 🌐 Until 1933, Papua New Guinea used seashells for money! Now they use Kina.

- 🌐 The world's first documented poisonous bird—the Hooded Pitohui—is native to Papua New Guinea.

Hooded Pitohui

Papua New Guinea

Travel with Mack and me to Arop at **wycliffe.org/A-Z**

8

B

Bwisi
(Bwi-si)

UGANDA

We've already made one friend, but we're just getting started! I want to introduce you to Dembe. He lives in Uganda. Dembe wants to tell us about what he wants to be when he grows up.

Wycliffe

Hi! My name is Dembe, and I want to be a pastor when I grow up, just like my dad. He's been a pastor my whole life, but he hasn't always had the Bible in Bwisi. That's the language we speak at home.

Dembe

When my dad was growing up, he didn't have a Bible he understood. He would listen to the Bible in English, but it wasn't the same. Sometimes it was hard to understand what the words really meant!

It wasn't until 1992 that missionaries started translating the Bible into the Bwisi language. It took many years of hard work, but now we have the whole New Testament!

My dad cried when he got his copy of the New Testament. I've never seen him so happy! He hugged the book to his chest and told me, "Now I can read God's Word in my heart language."

I was confused. "What's a heart language, Dad?"

He told me that my heart language is the language I dream in, think in, and talk to God in. Even though I speak English at school, I speak Bwisi at home with my family. When I dream, it's in Bwisi. And when I thought about it, I realized I talk to God in Bwisi too!

That day I realized that I had been given the best gift ever. Now I can read the Bible in my own language,

Dembe's Dad

Biblio Takirita

10

and I want to share it with everyone I know. When I get older, I want to become a pastor so that I can tell people how much Jesus loves them. He even speaks their heart language!

mountain gorilla & baby

FUN FACTS:

🌍 English is the official language of Uganda.

🌍 Nearly one-fifth of Uganda is open water or swampland!

🌍 Almost half of Lake Victoria, the biggest lake in Africa, is in Uganda.

Uganda

Kenya

Tanzania

Lake Victoria

🌍 Most of the endangered mountain gorillas are from Uganda. There are only around 750 left in the world!

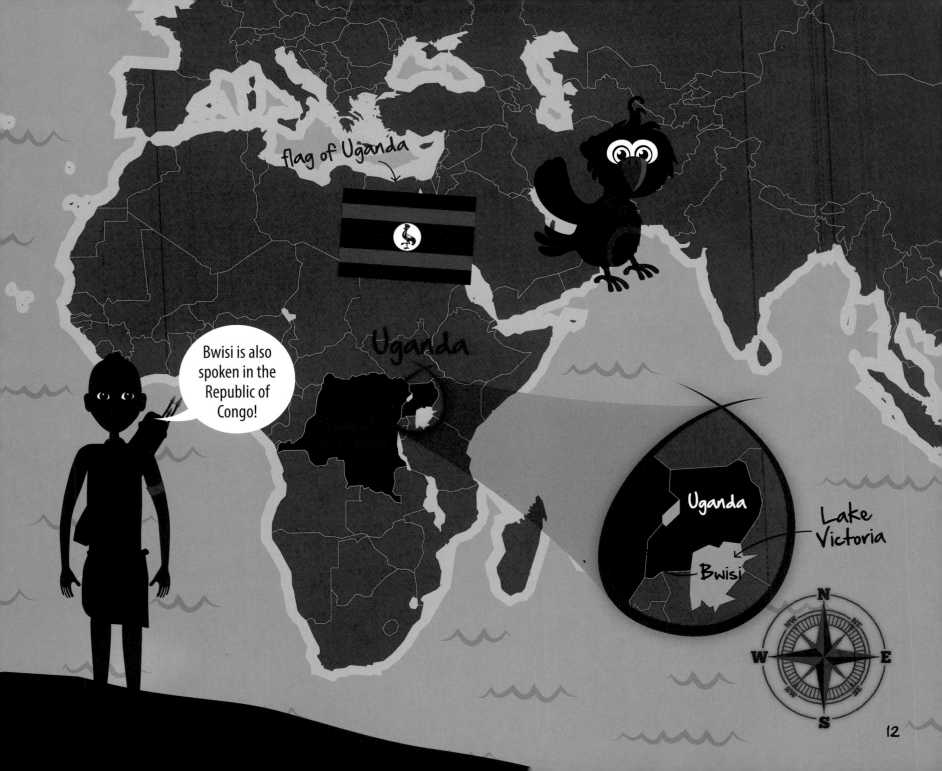

C

Catalan Sign Language

(Kae-tuh-lahn)

Did you know that there are over 200 different sign languages in the world? That's a lot! Not everyone understands American Sign Language, just like not everyone understands English.

Many deaf people use sign languages to communicate. Mack and I wondered if they could read the Bible if it was translated into the written language of their area. But then we found out that they might not learn how to read a written language, like English. It's important for a Deaf community to be able to have the Bible in the language that they speak—their sign language!

That's why we went to Spain, to learn about the Catalan Sign Language translation. There are around 18,000 people that speak Catalan Sign Language, and some of them use Spanish Sign Language too. They don't have the whole Bible yet, but exciting new things are happening!

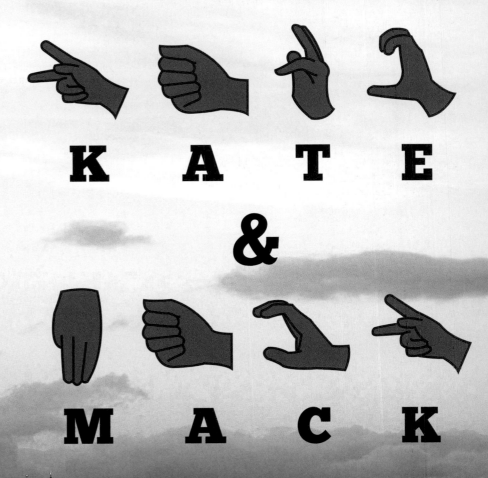

K A T E
&
M A C K

↖ Catalan Sign Language

Stories from the Bible are being made in 3-D. Do you know what 3-D means, Mack? It's where they make a cartoon person look like they're in the same room as you. That way it's as if you're talking to someone who is right there with you!

Because sign language uses your hands and the expressions on your face, it's important that the translations are able to show all that is going on. 3-D helps make that easier.

Now people are learning stories about Jesus in Catalan Sign Language. They can watch the movie clips and learn about the Bible. That's exciting news!

3-D Mack

Regular Mack

FUN FACTS:

🌍 The name "Spain" comes from the word *Ispania,* which means "the land of the rabbits."

🌍 Spain is the largest producer of bananas in Europe—almost 90 percent total.

🌍 Spain produces almost 45 percent of all olive oil in the world!

🌍 Football (what we call soccer in America) is the most popular sport in Spain.

Catalan flag

Spain

flag of Spain

Catalonia

16

Daakaka is an endangered language in Vanuatu. Do you know what it means when a language is endangered, Mack? It means there aren't many people who can speak it anymore.

Instead of learning Daakaka, most children grow up speaking the national language called Bislama. Only around 1,000 people are still alive who know how to speak Daakaka, and they live on an island called Ambrym. If something doesn't change soon, people won't know how to speak Daakaka anymore!

A natural disaster is something like a flood, a typhoon (that's a really big rain storm!), a tornado, or a huge fire. The island where Daakaka is spoken has an active volcano on it. That means it could erupt at any time, and people might have to move away to stay safe! If they move away, it could be to a place where people speak a different

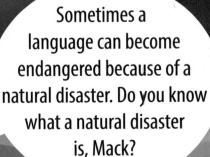

Sometimes a language can become endangered because of a natural disaster. Do you know what a natural disaster is, Mack?

language, and that's another way Daakaka might be forgotten.

Sometimes people who speak an endangered language might not get the Bible in their heart language. They may have the Bible in another language they speak instead. You can pray that the people who speak endangered languages would know that God loves them very much!

FUN FACTS:

- Vanuatu is made of 13 larger islands and around 70 smaller ones.

- There are more than 4,000 species of mollusks in Vanuatu.

- Most of the islands are mountainous and were made from volcanoes. Some of those volcanoes are still active, like on Ambrym!

- In Vanuatu, pigs (especially ones with round tusks) are considered a symbol of wealth.

Vanuatu pig ↘

mollusks ↘

19

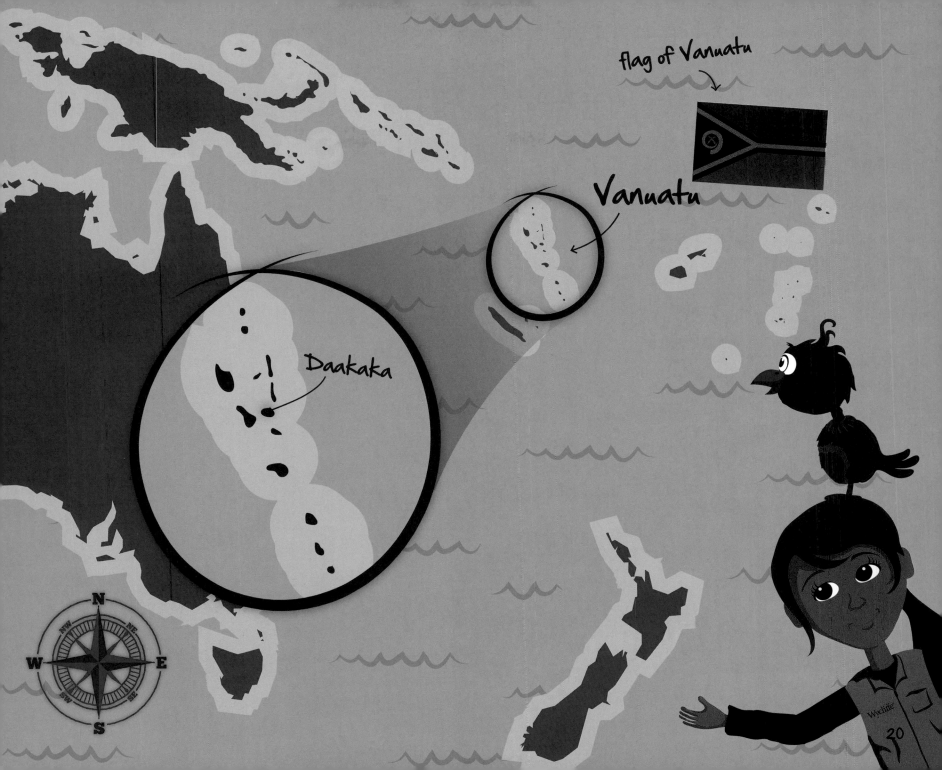

flag of Vanuatu

Vanuatu

Daakaka

Eastern Apurímac Quechua

(Ah-puu-ree-mac Ketch-wa)

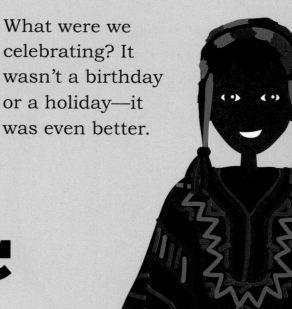

Luis

Hi! I'm Luis, and I want to tell you about the day I got my favorite book.

It was a really exciting day. We'd been preparing for months, and now we could finally celebrate!

What were we celebrating? It wasn't a birthday or a holiday—it was even better.

It was the day the Eastern Apurímac Quechua New Testament was dedicated!

I remember the first time I got to touch a copy of the new book. I'd been learning to read my language, but some words were still hard for me. I couldn't wait to practice by reading my new Bible.

I hugged the book to my chest, and then I carefully set it down in my lap. I slowly opened the cover and touched the first page. Then I put my finger under the top line of words and began to read. It was the very first time I read the Bible in my own language!

Now I get to read the Bible every day. I try to take very good care of my Bible, because it is my favorite book. And the day that I got my Bible was the happiest day of my life so far, because I was finally able to read it for myself!

One of the first verses that Luis read in his new Bible was John 3:16. Here's what it looks like in Eastern Apurímac Quechua!

Juan 3:16 "Diosqa ancha-anchatan kay pachapi runakunata munakuran. Chaymi sapallan Wawanta kay pachaman mandamuran, pipas paypi creeqqa ama wañunanpaq, aswanpas wiñay kawsayniyoq kananpaq."

FUN FACTS:

◍ In the Andes mountains (the second-highest mountain range in the world) there is a plant called Puya raimondii that has to grow for a hundred years before it gets flowers!

Puya raimondii

32 feet tall!

4 feet 10 inches tall!

◍ The highest sand dune in the world is in Peru. Cerro Blanco is 3,860 feet from the top to the bottom.

◍ The potato is originally from Peru. There are over 3,000 different kinds of potatoes.

◍ Cotahuasi Canyon is considered one of the world's deepest canyons. At 11,597 feet, it's twice as deep as the Grand Canyon!

24

F

Farefare
(Fa-rih-fa-rih)
GHANA

Hi, I'm Kojo. I speak the Farefare language. So do about 845,000 other people! Most live in Ghana, but some live in Burkina Faso too. That's the country just north of Ghana.

You want to hear something exciting? In 2008 we got the whole Bible. Now we can read what God has said from Genesis all the way to Revelation, in Farefare!

But although we have the whole Bible in our language, not everyone can read it. Some people had a really great idea.

Kojo

Meet Kojo. He lives in Ghana. Did you know it's popular in Ghana to name your baby after the day of the week they are born on? Kojo means "Monday," because that's the day he was born. That's a pretty cool fact!

Wycliffe

giant swallowtail butterfly

They thought, "What if people who can't read could listen to the Bible on the radio or watch a movie about Jesus' life?"

That movie is called the "JESUS" film, and it is being made in many different languages around the world. And stories from the Bible have been recorded so people can listen to them, just like you might listen to stories your mom or dad reads to you. More and more people are learning how much God loves them, even if they can't read. That's a wonderful thing!

FUN FACTS:

🌍 Six national parks and many smaller national preserves were set up to help protect Ghana's wildlife. In the Kakum National Park, there are over 650 butterfly species, including the giant swallowtails that are nearly eight inches from wing tip to wing tip!

🌍 There used to be a lot of elephants, leopards, wild buffalo, and antelope across Ghana, but now they are mostly found in nature reserves.

🌍 Deadly snakes such as the cobra, puff adder, and python are native to Ghana. Pythons aren't poisonous like the cobra and puff adder, but their strong muscles make them very dangerous.

🌍 The clothes that people traditionally wear in Ghana are made from bright and colorful kente cloth. Like Kojo's outfit!

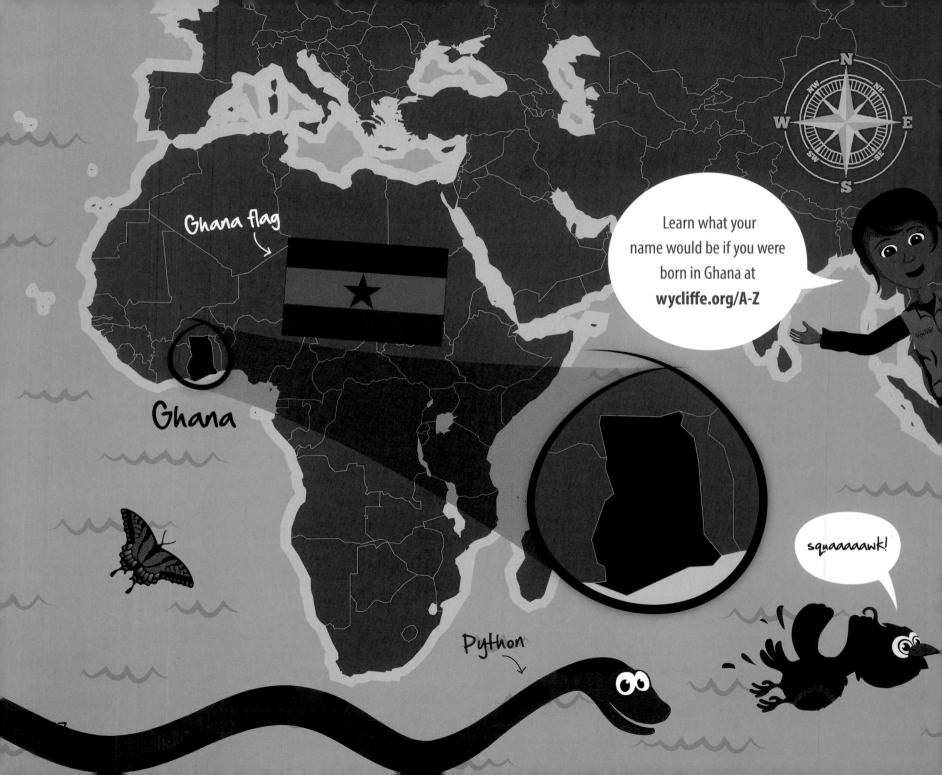

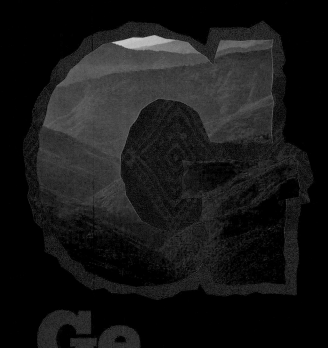

Ge
(Guh)
CHINA

Many languages around the world don't have the Bible. At Wycliffe, we call these "Bibleless people groups."

Did you know that even English was once a Bibleless people group? It was! The Bible was first written in Hebrew, Greek, and Aramaic and wasn't translated into other languages for many years. It wasn't until the 1300s that a man named John Wycliffe translated the Bible into English for the first time! So if you think about it, all languages have been Bibleless at some point in their history.

תנ"ך קדוש

"Holy Bible" in Hebrew ↗

The Ge language in China is one of those groups that still needs a Bible translation. In 1937, the Ge people received some portions of the Bible, but they need to have more.

Wycliffe

The Ge people can watch the "JESUS" film, because it has been recorded in their language. That way, they can learn about Jesus's life in their own language.

But this is just the start. It's really important that the Ge people get the Bible in their language. That way, they can learn more about God and how much He loves them. You can pray that Bibleless people groups like the Ge get the Bible soon!

giant panda

FUN FACTS:

🌐 The giant panda lives in the misty mountains of southwest China. It lives nowhere else on earth! Sadly pandas have been hunted so much that now only 1,600 remain in the wild.

🌐 The Great Wall of China is the largest man-made structure in the world. At 5,500 miles long, it could stretch from Los Angeles to New York, and back, and there would still be some left over!

The Great Wall of China

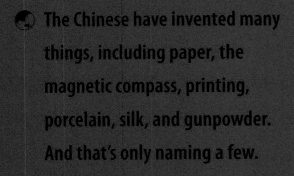

- The Chinese have invented many things, including paper, the magnetic compass, printing, porcelain, silk, and gunpowder. And that's only naming a few.

- With a population of 1.3 billion, China has more people than any other country on earth.

Play Sudoku, a game invented in China, at **wycliffe.org/A-Z**

China flag

China

Guizhou Province

Ge

N
NW NE
W E
SW SE
S

H

Huarijío
(Whahr-ee-he-o)

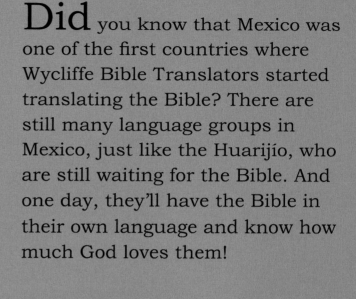

Did you know that Mexico was one of the first countries where Wycliffe Bible Translators started translating the Bible? There are still many language groups in Mexico, just like the Huarijío, who are still waiting for the Bible. And one day, they'll have the Bible in their own language and know how much God loves them!

The Huarijío language is spoken in Mexico, and people who speak Huarijío have portions of the Bible already. The whole New Testament is on its way, so the Huarijío people will soon be able to read about all of Jesus's life in their own language!

FUN FACTS:

- A Mexican tamale called the zacahuil is three feet long and weighs about 150 pounds.

- The Chihuahua is the world's smallest dog and is named after a Mexican state.

- In Mexico, children don't receive presents on Christmas Day. Instead, they receive gifts on January 6, El Día De Los Reyes (Three Kings' Day), celebrating the arrival of the wise men.

- Mexico introduced the world to chocolate, corn, and chilies.

flag of Mexico

Huarijío

Mexico

Chihuahua

zacahuil

Thank you, Mexico!

32

Ik
(Ick)

UGANDA

Kitella

Hello, my name is Kitella. I'm from an Ik village in Uganda. I don't have the Bible.

My people are isolated. That means we live far away from other people and from cities. Many wars have happened in our country, especially in the northern part of Uganda. That's where I live. War can make people more isolated, and it can be tough to know if people need a Bible if they're hard to find!

My family and I speak Ik, but our language is still being developed. That means people are writing down and recording our language so it won't be forgotten or stop being used. If people quit using it, then no one will be able to read the Bible in Ik.

But many people cannot read or write yet. Hopefully one day we will know how, and we will have the Bible in Ik too!

Lots of people are Christians in Uganda. That's how I heard about Jesus. I love Him very much, but sometimes it is hard because I don't always understand what the pastor is saying about Jesus.

Having a Bible in our own language would be very good for my people. Then we would finally be able to clearly understand what God is saying to us. It would be like He was speaking right to me, Kitella!

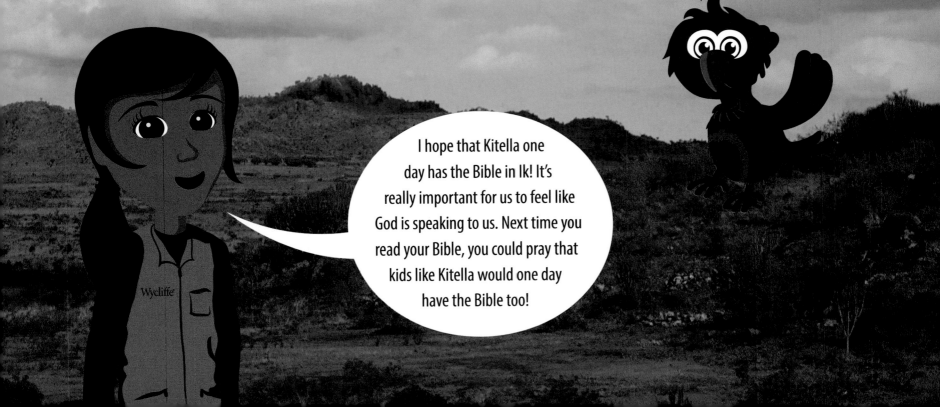

I hope that Kitella one day has the Bible in Ik! It's really important for us to feel like God is speaking to us. Next time you read your Bible, you could pray that kids like Kitella would one day have the Bible too!

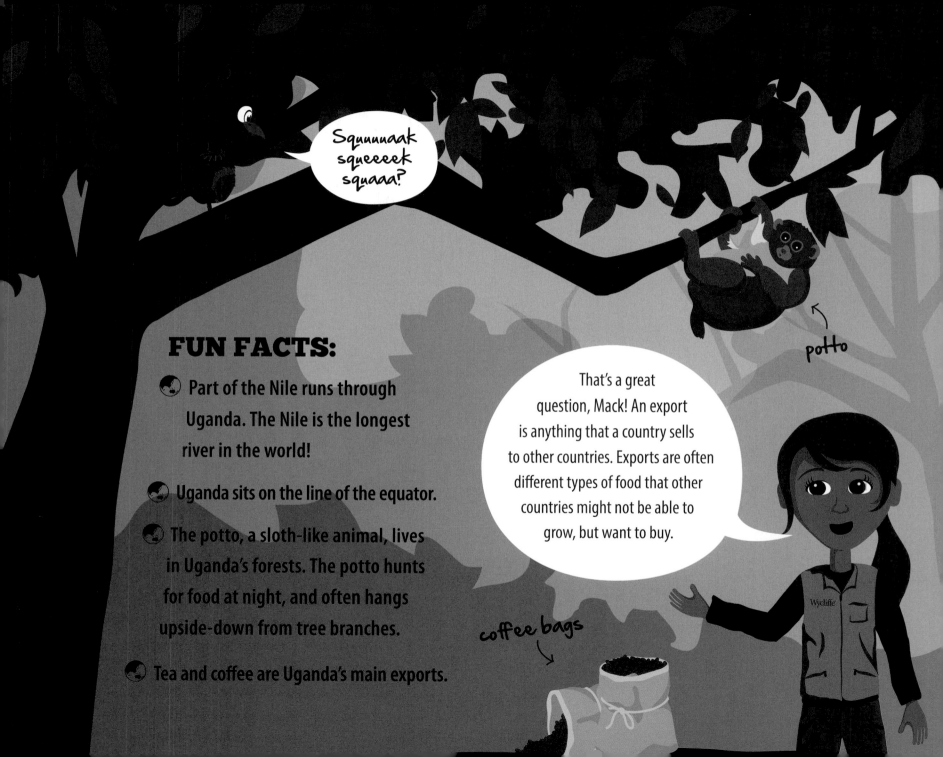

Squuuuak squeeeek squaaa?

FUN FACTS:

🌍 Part of the Nile runs through Uganda. The Nile is the longest river in the world!

🌍 Uganda sits on the line of the equator.

🌍 The potto, a sloth-like animal, lives in Uganda's forests. The potto hunts for food at night, and often hangs upside-down from tree branches.

🌍 Tea and coffee are Uganda's main exports.

That's a great question, Mack! An export is anything that a country sells to other countries. Exports are often different types of food that other countries might not be able to grow, but want to buy.

potto

coffee bags

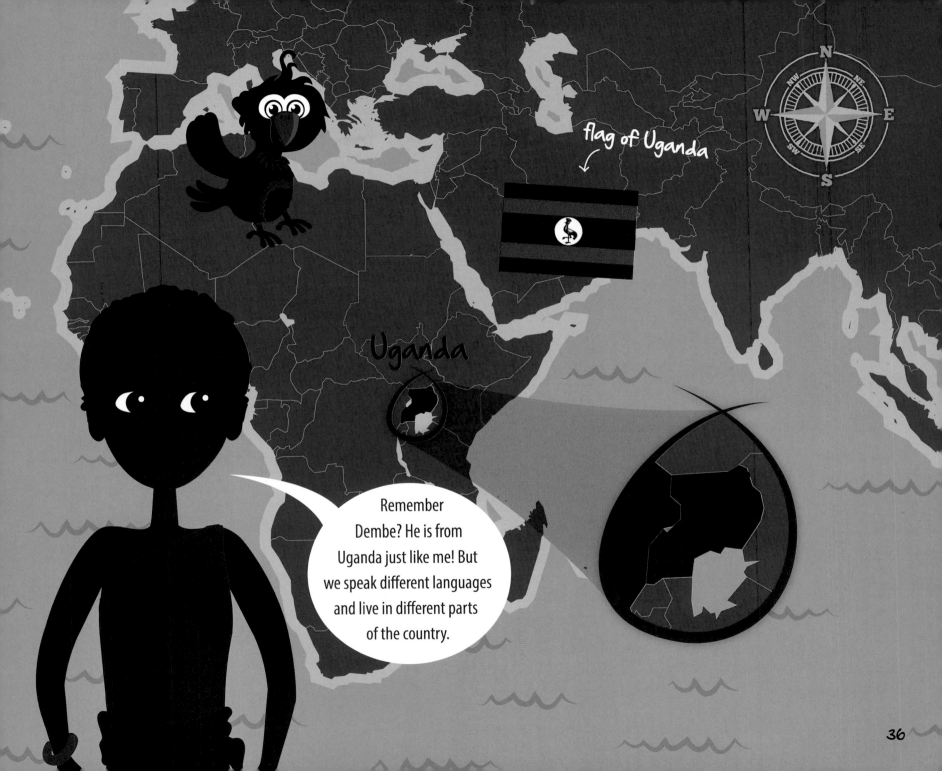

flag of Uganda

Uganda

Remember Dembe? He is from Uganda just like me! But we speak different languages and live in different parts of the country.

Japanese Sign Language

JAPAN

Did you know that there are over 100 different deaf schools that use Japanese Sign Language to teach students? That's a really good thing, because now most deaf people in Japan understand it. But they still need to understand how much God loves them. That's why there is a group of people working on making videos of Bible stories in Japanese Sign Language. They call it ViBi, a short name for Video Bible!

Remember when we talked about the Catalan Sign Language in Spain, Mack? Now we're going to learn about Japanese Sign Language!

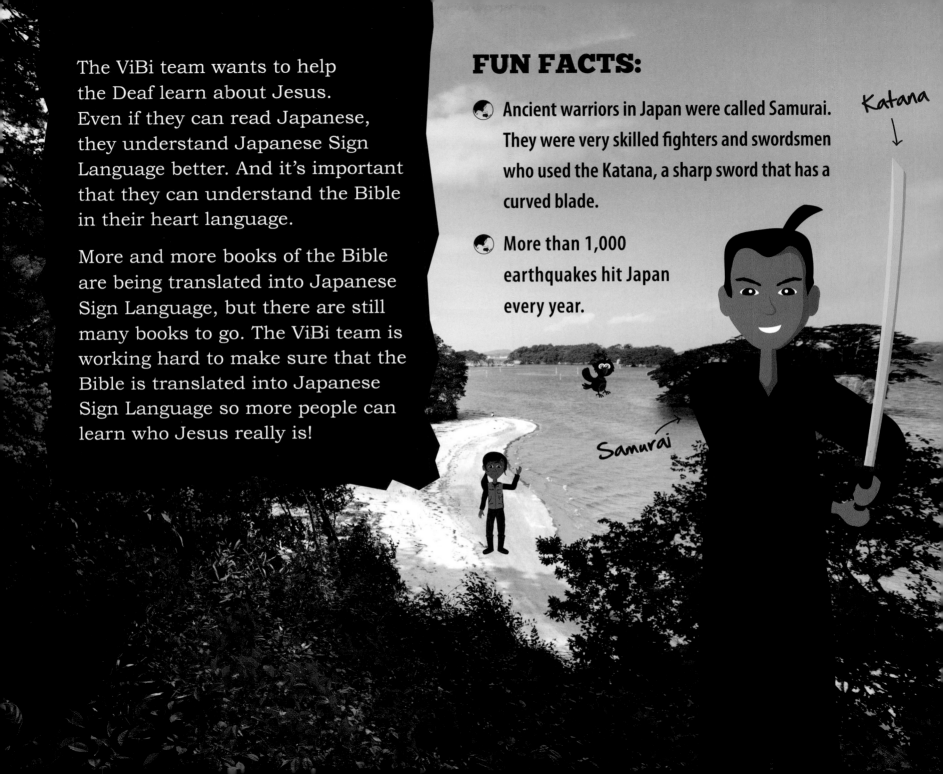

The ViBi team wants to help the Deaf learn about Jesus. Even if they can read Japanese, they understand Japanese Sign Language better. And it's important that they can understand the Bible in their heart language.

More and more books of the Bible are being translated into Japanese Sign Language, but there are still many books to go. The ViBi team is working hard to make sure that the Bible is translated into Japanese Sign Language so more people can learn who Jesus really is!

FUN FACTS:

- Ancient warriors in Japan were called Samurai. They were very skilled fighters and swordsmen who used the Katana, a sharp sword that has a curved blade.

- More than 1,000 earthquakes hit Japan every year.

Katana
↓

Samurai

There are around 200 volcanoes in Japan, and 60 of them are active. Mount Fuji is one of them!

Sumo wrestling is a national sport, but baseball is the most popular sport to watch.

flag of Japan

Japan

Mount Fuji

K

Khaling
(Kah-ling)

Hello, my name is Raju. I live in Nepal, and I speak Khaling. We have the whole Bible in our language, and that makes us very excited! But it wasn't easy to get the Bible. In fact, it took over 40 years!

Raju

40

Tim and Ingrid Toba were the first missionaries to come work with the Khaling language. In 1970 they moved to Nepal. But before they could even begin translating, they had to study Khaling. Then they worked on translating the Bible.

When Tim and Ingrid tried to share the Bible with the people, no one wanted to listen! They were all too busy working in the fields. They didn't understand why Tim and Ingrid had time to read when there was so much work to be done.

Another hard thing was that back then, girls did not go to school. That meant that a lot of people couldn't read or write.

Tim and Ingrid kept trying, but soon they faced another problem. After only six years of work, they had to leave Nepal. The government decided they didn't want any foreigners in their country anymore. So they left, wondering what would happen to the Khaling project!

Eight years passed. Tim and Ingrid lived in other countries, but they kept working on translating the Bible into Khaling. One night, three young

Tim & Ingrid around 1970

Tim & Ingrid around 2011

Khaling men were baptized. And that's when things started to change.

More people became interested in who God was and wanted to believe. As more people heard about Jesus, they would tell their neighbors what they had learned. And soon, Tim and Ingrid were working with some Khaling people to translate the whole New Testament.

In 1994, the Khaling New Testament was printed. Everyone was really excited! But they wanted more—they wanted the Old Testament too! And first, they wanted to be able to read the book of Psalms.

One of the young men who had been baptized was named Simon. He was in charge of the team that worked on translating the Old Testament. The team worked hard for a lot of years. Finally, in 2011, the whole Bible in Khaling was finished!

I was only five years old when the Bible was completed, so I didn't have to wait very long at all. In fact, I can't remember ever not having the Bible! But my mom and dad were just my age when Tim and Ingrid first started translating. They waited their whole lives for the Bible, and now we finally have it! That makes us all very happy.

FUN FACTS:

- The Yeti (or Abominable Snowman) is believed to live in the mountains of Nepal. No one has ever found the Yeti, but some people say they've seen its footprints.

- Nepal has the biggest altitude change on earth. The lowlands are at sea level, and the Himalayan mountains are the tallest on earth. In fact, eight of the world's 10 tallest mountain peaks are in Nepal, including Mount Everest, the tallest mountain in the world!

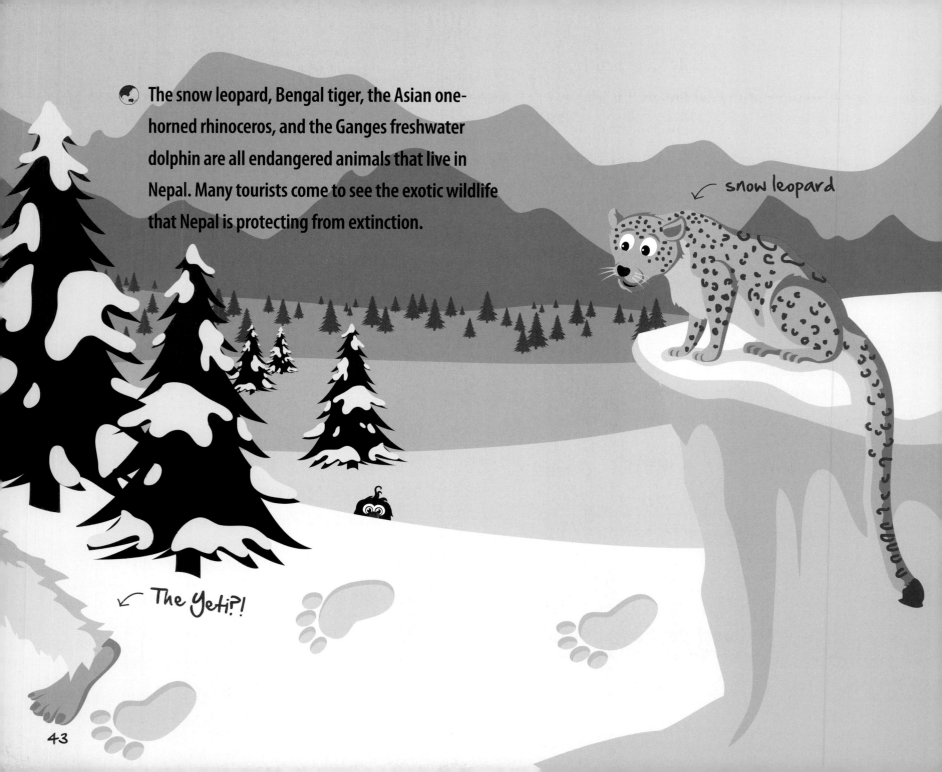

The snow leopard, Bengal tiger, the Asian one-horned rhinoceros, and the Ganges freshwater dolphin are all endangered animals that live in Nepal. Many tourists come to see the exotic wildlife that Nepal is protecting from extinction.

snow leopard

The Yeti?!

43

Livvi-Karelian
(Lih-vee Kah-ree-li-an)

Some languages are spoken in more than one country. Think of English or Spanish—they're spoken in a lot of different countries! Languages spread like this when people move to a new place and take their language with them. When they move as a big group, it's called migration. That's what happened with the Livvi-Karelian language. Although most people who speak Livvi-Karelian live in the Russian Federation, some of them moved to Finland many years ago.

45

The good news is that the whole New Testament has been translatedfor people who speak Livvi-Karelian!

Translation of parts of the Bible first started way back in 1800s. But it wasn't until 2003 that they finally got the New Testament. That's a long time to wait, isn't it, Mack?

Remember the story of Jesus' birth? People waited a long time for Jesus to be born. And lots of people are waiting a long time to read that story in their own language. Find Luke 2:1–7 in your Bible and read it.

The words make sense to you, because you have learned to read them. But this is what some of that story looks like in Livvi-Karelian:

Did you understand any of this? I don't, but I know that people who speak and read Livvi-Karelian do! That's why it's so important to have the Bible in your own language—so you can understand and read it for yourself.

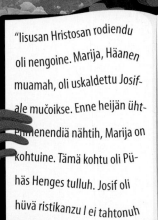

"Iisusan Hristosan rodiendu oli nengoine. Marija, Häanen muamah, oli uskaldettu Josif-ale mučoikse. Enne heijän üht-enmenendiä nähtih, Marija on kohtuine. Tämä kohtu oli Pü-häs Henges tulluh. Josif oli hüvä ristikanzu I ei tahtonuh huijata hänele uskaldettuu Marijua rahvahan ies, a ta-htoi hil'l'azeh jättiä hän Konzu Josif duuma- iččiu sudä üöl unis tuli hänen luo Tai- vahallizen lžändäan an-heli da sanoi: Josif, Davidan poigu, älä varua ottua Marijua

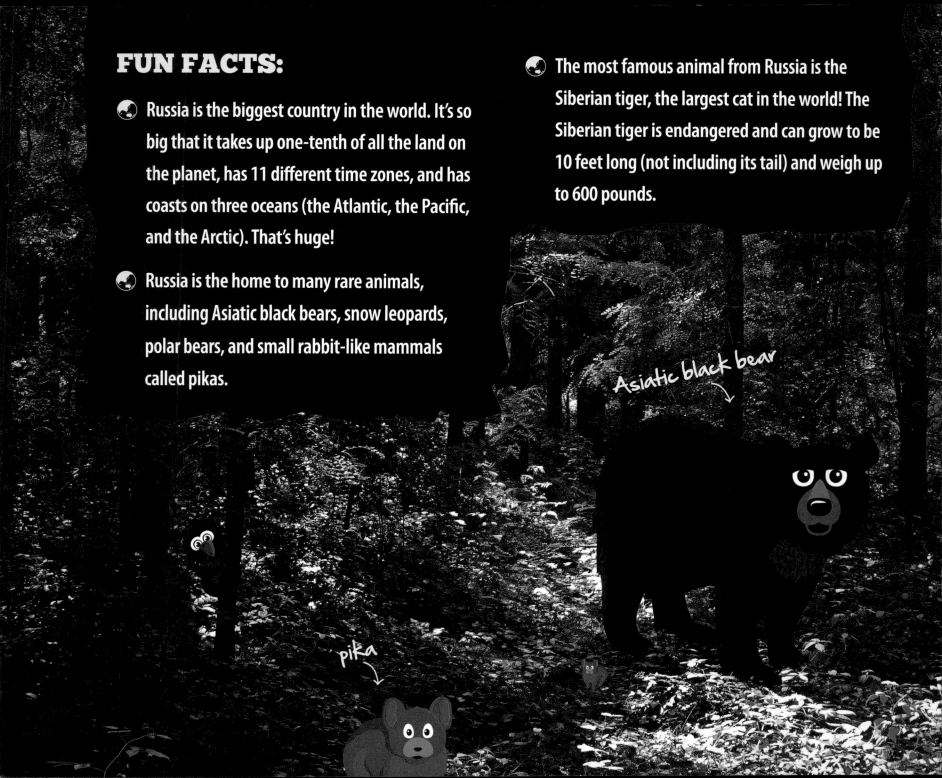

FUN FACTS:

🌏 Russia is the biggest country in the world. It's so big that it takes up one-tenth of all the land on the planet, has 11 different time zones, and has coasts on three oceans (the Atlantic, the Pacific, and the Arctic). That's huge!

🌏 Russia is the home to many rare animals, including Asiatic black bears, snow leopards, polar bears, and small rabbit-like mammals called pikas.

🌏 The most famous animal from Russia is the Siberian tiger, the largest cat in the world! The Siberian tiger is endangered and can grow to be 10 feet long (not including its tail) and weigh up to 600 pounds.

Asiatic black bear

pika

Finland

Sputnik

flag of Finland

flag of Russia

🌐 The first satellite to go into space was launched from Russia in 1957. It was named Sputnik.

Wycliffe

48

Marma
(Mar-ma)
BANGLADESH

There are over 180,500 people who speak Marma in Bangladesh, but very few believe in Jesus. A Bible translation can help them learn who Jesus is and how much God loves them. If they don't know that, they might not know that they can love Him back.

God wants us to know Him. That's why He had people throughout history write down messages from Him. And when all those messages are brought together, we have a whole Bible!

In the future, the Marma people will be able to hold the Bible in their hands and know about God. It might take years of hard work, but God is good and wants everyone to know Him. And one day, all their hard work will help make the Bible available in Marma. Let's pray that day comes soon!

FUN FACTS:

- The Royal Bengal tiger is the national animal of Bangladesh, but it's endangered now. The tiger's roar can be heard from almost two miles away!

- Bangladesh has six different seasons each year. It's sometimes called "the playground of seasons." The seasons are named grismo (summer), barsha (rainy), sharat, (autumn), hemanto (cool), sheet (winter), and bashonto (spring).

Royal Bengal tiger

Bangladesh is one of the most crowded countries on earth, with more than 2,600 people per square mile. That's a lot of people for a small space!

People in Bangladesh think that if you smile a lot, you are immature. So even when people are friendly, they may not smile very much!

flag of Bangladesh

Bangladesh

Make *paratha*, a Bangladeshi flatbread, at **wycliffe.org/A-Z**

Marma

Nadëb
(Naa deeb)
BRAZIL

Hi, my name is Felipe! I'm from a people group called the Nadëb. We live deep in the Amazon rainforest of Brazil. And by deep, I mean deeeeeeep. We're one of the most isolated people groups in Brazil!

It takes a lot of hard work and time to reach our home. There are no roads, and paths can be very hard to find and follow. There are even parts of the jungle that no one has ever been through before! But thankfully some missionaries made the long, hard journey to find us and help us get God's Word in Nadëb.

Those missionaries are named Rodolfo and Beatrice Senn. Before they came, we didn't know that there was someone out there who thought we were important enough to send His only Son to save us—God!

But Rodolfo and Beatrice helped us know Jesus. They worked for 16 years before they finished translating the New Testament.

Badäk hahỹỹh, wë na-ããj da ahëëj jëë né paawä, kĕh ỹỹ da dooh tahëëj bä

As we learned more about God, we realized that we wanted to know Him. We wanted to find joy in Him! Following Jesus would be our new goal in life.

We were all very excited the day the New Testament was dedicated. We sang and danced and laughed. Everyone was filled with joy because we finally had the Bible.

We even made special shirts in bright colors for people to wear—orange, red, pink, blue, and purple. On the front of the shirts, we wrote Matthew 24:35 in our language, which says, "Badäk hahỹỹh, wë na-ããj da ahëëj jëë né paawä, kĕh ỹỹ da dooh tahëëj bä." In English it reads, "Heaven and earth will disappear, but my words will never disappear." That is a verse we always want to remember!

FUN FACTS:

- Brazil is the biggest country in South America. It's also the fifth largest nation in the world, and it borders every country in South America except Chile and Ecuador—10 countries!

- The Amazon River and the jungles that surround it fill most of Northern Brazil. Did you know the Amazon is actually a network of hundreds of waterways stretching for 4,250 miles? That makes it the longest river on Earth!

- Thousands of animal species live in the Amazon River, including the piranha and the boto, a pink river dolphin.

- Brazil has a greater variety of living creatures than any other country in the world. There are 600 kinds of mammals, 1,500 kinds of fish, 1,600 kinds of birds, and 100,000 kinds of insects that live there! Most of these creatures live in the jungles, such as the Amazon Rainforest.

piranha

boto

Owa
(OH-wah)
SOLOMON ISLANDS

Isabel

Hi, kids! Have you ever heard of the Solomon Islands before? It's a small country in the Pacific Ocean, near Australia and Papua New Guinea.

Anyway, I'm going to tell you a little about my language. It's called Owa. And I'm Isabel, by the way. I'm so excited that you're learning about my people!

We have the whole New Testament in Owa, and more and more of us are taking classes to learn to read and write. The exciting thing is that as we learn how to read, we get to learn from the Bible itself!

I go to classes every week, and my mom goes with me. Before these classes, my mom didn't know how to read. But now that people are teaching classes, we both get to learn! She's learning really fast, and she loves reading the Bible. It's one of her favorite things to do.

My mom wants to learn how to read so well that, one day, she can be a teacher and help other people learn how to read and write Owa. And most importantly, she wants to help them learn how to read the Bible in Owa. Maybe I will teach one day too, when I'm older!

FUN FACTS:

🌐 People in the Solomon Islands are trying to help save the endangered leatherback turtle, one of the largest turtles on earth! It can grow up to seven feet long and weigh more than 2,000 pounds. Leatherback turtles can dive up to 4,200 feet deep—deeper than any other turtle—and can stay underwater for up to 85 minutes.

leatherback turtle

Solomon Islands

I live on the tip of that island!

Owa

There are only two seasons in the Solomon Islands—dry and rainy.

The world's largest salt water lagoon is in New Georgia, Solomon Islands, and it's called the Marovo Lagoon.

The Solomon Islands is made up of six main islands, which are all volcanic, and nearly 1,000 smaller islands.

flag of Solomon Islands

Pouye

(BOO-yay)

Hi, kids! My name is Joseph, and I live in Papua New Guinea. Kate told me that you've been to my country before and met Anna, who speaks Arop. You might think that since we live in the same country, we'd speak the same language. But there are over 800 different languages in our country! I speak a language called Pouye.

Joseph ↙

Even though there are only about 1,000 people that speak Pouye, a Bible is being translated for us! Many of us also speak Tok Pisin. That's a language lots of people speak in Papua New Guinea. It's what you would call a trade language—a language that's used when doing business.

Even though a lot of the Bible is translated into Tok Pisin, it's harder for us to understand. Since Tok Pisin is mainly for doing business, it doesn't have a lot of familiar words for things found in the Bible, so sometimes we get confused. And when we get confused, we might miss some of what God is trying to say to us!

In Pouye the word for "God" is *Irpapowiyu Ramu*. When you translate that back into English, it basically means "Creator Being." God created everything in this whole world—including all the languages! The reason it's so important that we have the Bible in Pouye is because God created our language too. And just like in the creation story in Genesis, God looked at what He had created and said, "It is good." I'm sure He says the same thing when He sees more people getting the Bible in the language their heart understands best.

FUN FACTS:

- People who speak Pouye often eat their food with a spoon, but they also use their hands.

- Papua New Guinea shares the island of New Guinea with Indonesia, and it's one of the biggest islands in the world! Only Greenland is bigger.

- The smallest frog in the world, called Paedophryne amauensis, was discovered in Papua New Guinea. It's around the size of a fly!

Paedophryne amauensis

60

bird of paradise

Over 400 different types of
birds live in Papua New Guinea,
including the bird of paradise,
the bowerbird, the cassowary,
the kingfisher, and the parrot.

kingfisher

bowerbird

parrot

Wycliffe

Translation work began for the Q'anjob'al people many years ago. Now they have the Bible, but it's not just written in a book—it's also recorded! Many people who speak Q'anjob'al aren't able to read, which makes the recorded Bible that much more special. Now they can learn about God too!

Quetzal bird

FUN FACTS:

🌐 Lake Atitlán is what is called a caldera—a lake that is formed when a volcano explodes and collapses. It's the deepest lake in Central America and is believed to be 1,000 feet deep and 48 square miles in size.

🌐 High in the mountains of Guatemala lives the Quetzal bird. Both the male and female have vibrant green, white, and red feathers, but only the male has the long tail that can reach up to three feet! It's now an endangered bird because of destruction to the tropical rainforest.

🌐 People believe that the name Guatemala comes from the old Mayan word *Guhatezmath*, which was used to describe a volcano. Translated into English, *Guhatezmath* means "Mountain that Vomits Water." Today people call volcanoes Volcán de Agua, which means "Volcano of Water."

Guatemala is one of the world's biggest providers of jade. Jade is a beautiful stone that comes from the mineral jadeite.

Guatemala

flag of Guatemala

Jade

Q'anjob'al

Rangi
(Rahn-ghee)
TANZANIA

Wycliffe

Salma

Hello, my name is Salma. I live in Tanzania. Kate and Mack told me about your trip around the world, and it sounds like so much fun! I know you've visited two other countries in Africa—Ghana and Uganda—but Africa is huge!

Did you know that there are 56 countries in Africa? That's a lot! I'm so excited that you have come to visit me in Tanzania and learn more about my language. It's called Rangi.

Sometimes languages have more than one name. And my language is one of them! Some people call my language "Langi," but people who speak Swahili call it "Rangi."

We don't have a printed Bible yet, but translation is happening! And every time I hear new verses read in Rangi, it makes my heart very happy. I cannot wait until we can have the whole New Testament. That will be a lot of verses to read!

FUN FACTS:

🌍 Mount Kilimanjaro in Tanzania was once an active volcano. It is the highest point in Africa. It's also near three of the largest lakes in Africa: Lake Victoria, Lake Tanganyika, and Lake Nyasa.

🌍 Wildebeests, zebras, giraffes, elephants, rhinos, lions, and leopards all live in Tanzania.

🌍 There are some big national parks in Tanzania! The Gombe Stream National Park is home to many chimpanzees. It is where Jane Goodall—a scientist—did 45 years of research on chimps in their natural habitat. The Serengeti National Park is the oldest and most popular park for tourists to visit. There are over 1.7 million wildebeest that live there, as well as about a million other animals!

Illegal hunting, killing, or capturing of wild animals is called poaching. That's another reason why animal reserves exist, to help protect animals and make sure their species stays alive.

67

Many elephants live in Tanzania's Selous Game Reserve. People at the reserve try to protect the elephants, but some hunters still kill them illegally for their ivory tusks.

wildebeest

elephant

68

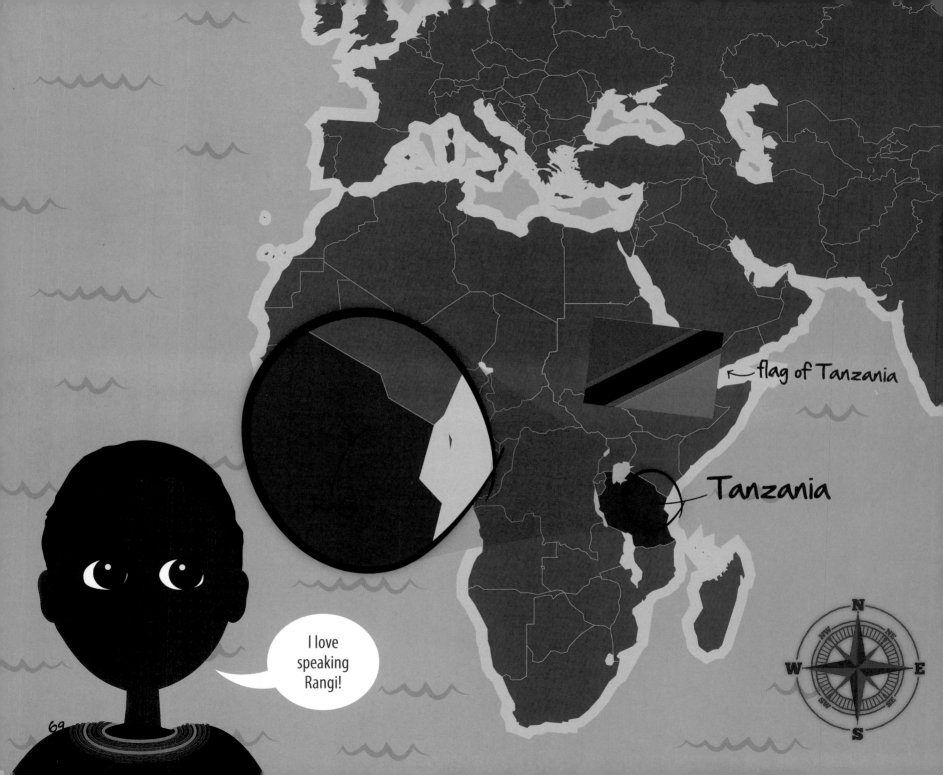

Sinte Romani
(SIN-tay ro-MAR-ni)

Luca

Hi, kids! My name is Luca. I speak Sinte Romani. I live in a country called Serbia, but people who speak my language live all across Europe. Whenever they move to new countries, they take the language with them.

We have a New Testament translated in our language. But since we don't all live in one area, some people who speak Sinte Romani still don't know about the translation. What a wonderful surprise it is when they see the Sinte Romani New Testament for the first time! When they are able to read the Bible in their heart language, it finally makes sense.

When I grow up, I hope that I can become a missionary to my own people. I'll travel all over and tell people who speak Sinte Romani that Jesus speaks their language too. And when they read the Bible in Sinte Romani, they might want to become a missionary too!

raspberries

FUN FACTS:

🌍 In Serbia, Christmas is celebrated on January 7. That's because Serbs use the Julian calendar, while many churches use the Gregorian calendar.

🌍 In Serbia, most last names end with the letters "ić." Some common last names are: Marković, Petrović, and Jovanović.

🌍 Most of the world's raspberries come from Serbia. In 2012, almost 95 percent of all raspberries came from Serbia!

🌍 A Serbian word that is used around the world is *vampire*.

Wycliffe

Tunia

(TOON-ee-ah)

Hi! I'm Nadia. I live in Chad, a country in Africa. I'm from the Tun people. We speak a language called Tunia.

There aren't very many people who still speak Tunia—less than 5,000! For a long time, our language didn't even have an alphabet. So we didn't know how to read or write Tunia.

Nadia

One day missionaries moved to our village to learn our language and help us get an alphabet. Their names are Samuel and Claudine Mbaihoguemel, and they are from Chad too!

Samuel and Claudine wanted to help us create an alphabet so that one day we could have the Bible. After all, how can you have the Bible written down if you don't even have an alphabet?

Now that we have an alphabet, the Bible can be translated for us. And one day, we'll finally be able to read it in Tunia!

FUN FACTS:

raptor

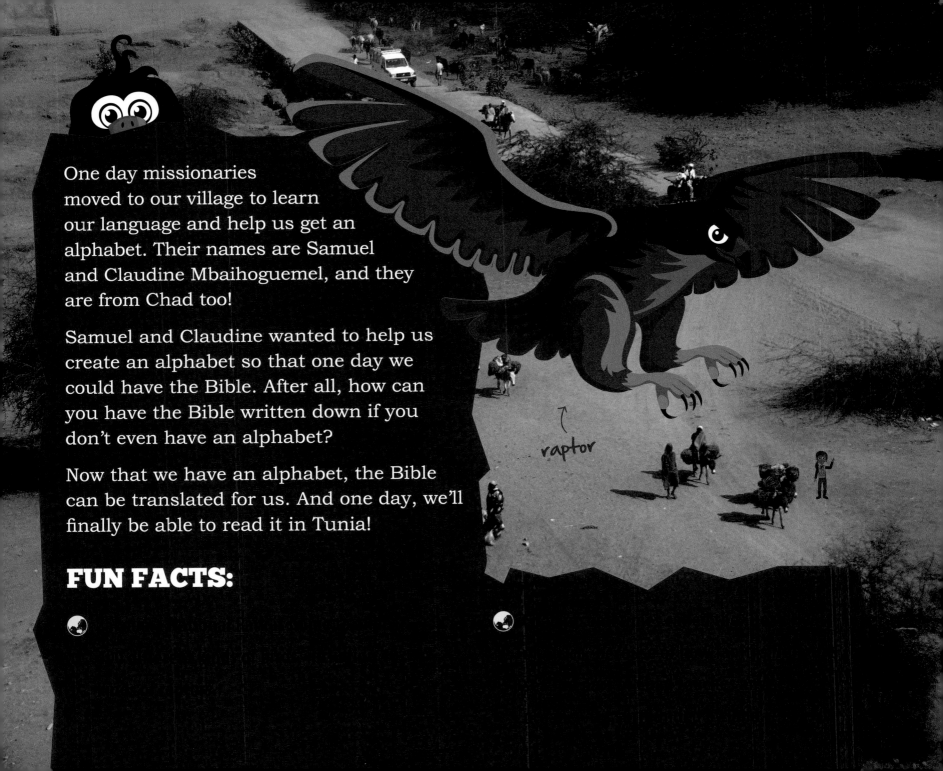

Around one-third of Chad is covered by the Sahara Desert. Even in the coldest part of the year, the Saharan portion of Chad stays around 90 degrees, and in the summer, temperatures rise to an average of 113 degrees. That's really hot!

The country of Chad got its name from a large lake just north of the capital city. Lake Chad is the country's greatest tourist attraction, and it is considered one of the most beautiful natural wonders of the world.

flag of Chad

Chad

That's my beautiful country!

Tunia

N
NW NE
W E
SW SE
S

Udmurt
(Ood-moort)
RUSSIA

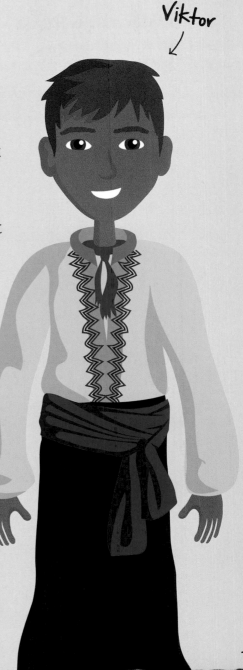

Viktor

Hello, my name is Viktor. I live in the Russian Federation. Kate and Mack told me that you've been to Russia before when you met the Livvi-Karelian people. So you probably already know that this is the biggest country in the world.

Since Russia is so big, there are a lot of different languages. My family and I speak a language called Udmurt. It's written in the Cyrillic alphabet. It looks very different from the Latin alphabet you use in English.

My *babushka*—that means grandmother, in Russian—waited almost her whole life for the Bible in her language. She's very old, so that's a long time to wait.

In fact, it took over 160 years to get the whole Udmurt Bible translated. Way back in 1847, the Gospel of Matthew was first published. Then in 1997 the New Testament was published. Finally, in November 2013, we were able to hold the whole Bible in our hands. All in one book!

We also have the "JESUS" film, and that's one of my favorite things to watch. It's very cool to hear Jesus talk in my own language. It makes me feel like He's talking right to me.

I learned in the Bible that God made all the languages in the world, and that Jesus wants everyone to know how much He loves them. But that can be hard to understand if the Bible is not in your language.

Next time you read your Bible or watch a movie about Jesus, remember that there are many more kids out there who are still waiting for a Bible. I try to remember that, because my own babushka didn't have the Bible for

АБВГДЕ
ЁЖЗИЙК
ЛМНОПР
СТУФХЦ
ЧШЩЪЫ
ЬЭЮЯ

Cyrillic

Latin

ABCDEF
GHIJKL
MNOPQ
RSTUV
WXYZ

Wycliffe

many years. I'm so glad that Jesus understands Udmurt, and that I can talk to Him in my own language whenever I want.

FUN FACTS:

- About three-fourths of Russia's land is in Siberia, a region covered mostly in sprawling pine forest called taiga. In fact, Siberia has close to 25 percent of all the forests in the world!

- In Russia, people don't like to shake hands across a doorway, because they believe it might cause arguments that will never end.

- The Russian State Library is the second-largest library in the world. The only library bigger is the Library of Congress in the United States.

- The Tsar-Kolokol is the largest bell in the world. It weighs 446,000 pounds (heavier than a blue whale!) and is over 20 feet tall. Only a little while after it was made, in 1753, it cracked and has never, ever been rung.

Tsar-Kolokol

Vaghri
(Bag-ree)
PAKISTAN

The Vaghri people live in the country of Pakistan. The name *Pakistan* means "land of the pure." People in Pakistan are often known for their hospitality, strong family values, and loyalty.

Most of the people who live in Pakistan are Muslim—about 97 percent. Less than 2 percent of the people claim to be Christian. And there aren't very many who have the Bible translated into their language.

People who speak Vaghri don't have any of the Bible in their language yet. More than 70 languages are spoken across Pakistan. The very first translation of a New Testament in Pakistan was dedicated in 1996, and some of the Bible has been translated into four other languages. Today there are Bible translations being done in over 20 different languages. That's around one-third of all the languages in Pakistan!

80

Some people in Pakistan might know of Jesus, but very few of them know that He loves them so much that He died on the cross for them. You can pray that more people would hear of Jesus and want a Bible for themselves. You can also pray that one day, the Vaghri people will know that Jesus loves them an awful lot.

FUN FACTS:

- Field hockey is Pakistan's national sport, and they're good at it! They won Olympic gold medals in 1960, 1968, and 1984, and the Hockey World Cup in 1971, 1978, 1982, and 1994.

- Of the 30 tallest mountain peaks across the planet, 13 of them are in Pakistan.

- The Tharparkar Desert in the south of Pakistan is the only fertile desert in the world.

- A city in Pakistan, called Sialkot, is the world's biggest producer of hand-stitched footballs (soccer balls).

field hockey stick and ball →

Pakistan

flag of Pakistan

Waata
(Wah-tah)
KENYA

Hi! My name is Zahra, and I live in Kenya. So far 17 languages in Kenya have the whole Bible, 13 have New Testaments, and 10 others have part of the Bible.

My language is called Waata. We don't have any of the Bible translated for us yet.

There is a Kenyan organization that is trying to get the Bible translated for more of the languages in Kenya. They want to bring God's Word to everyone in our country who doesn't have it yet—like my language!

Zahra

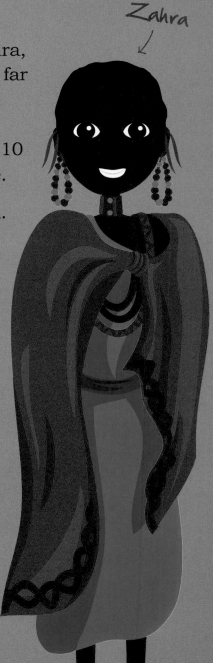

I've heard that around the world, more and more people are working to help translate the Bible in their own language. They're often called mother tongue translators. And they are really helpful, since they already know the language and the culture!

I've heard some of the Bible in English and Swahili, but it doesn't always make sense to me in those languages.

I think that when I grow up, I want to be a translator. Maybe I'll even be able to help translate the Bible for my own people! But if the Bible is already in Waata by the time I'm all grown up, I want to help other languages get the Bible. That way they'll be able to read it in their own language and not just in a second or third language they might speak!

FUN FACTS:

🌍 There are more than 60 languages in Kenya. Most people speak more than one African language.

🌍 The Great Rift Valley is a 4,000 mile tear in the crust of the earth. That's really long!

🌍 Kenya is known for its fast runners, who often win medals at the Olympics in track and field events. Out of the 86 metals that Kenyan athletes have won at the Olympics, 56 of them are in long-distance running.

rhino

There are more than 50 reserves and parks in Kenya that are home to animals such as giraffes, rhinos, elephants, lions, cheetahs, zebras, hippos, and many more. And in Kenya's highland forests live many animals that are found nowhere else in the world.

giraffes

Some languages are in places where people aren't allowed to talk about Jesus. Or maybe some don't want Bible translation to happen there. When we talk about these languages, we have to use pseudonyms. That way we can tell their stories and not say who they are or where they live.

The next time you see a language with a pseudonym—like Language X—you can pray for the people! Pray for the missionaries who are working there, and pray that people would be excited about the Bible being translated into their language. Pray that they would want to read it and learn about Jesus. That way, they can know how much He loves them!

Have you ever seen a language that doesn't have a name? Maybe people just call it by a letter, like "Language X." Or maybe they use a fake name. That's called a pseudonym.

Wycliffe

Yopno

(YOPE-no)

PAPUA NEW GUINEA

Peter

Hello, kids! My name is Peter. Welcome back to Papua New Guinea! Kate says this is the third time you've visited my country. You might wonder why you've been here so many times, but I might have an idea why.

Did you know that there are over 800 different languages spoken in Papua New Guinea? That's an awful lot! And did you know that over 300 languages still don't have even one verse of the Bible translated for them? Papua New Guinea has the second-highest number of Bible translation needs in the world.

Even though there are so many languages still waiting, the Bible is available in more languages in Papua New Guinea than any other country in the world. It's cool to see how more and more people are getting the Bible every day!

My language is called Yopno, and we have the book of Psalms and the New Testament in our language. I was a little boy when the New Testament was printed in Yopno in 2010. I couldn't read, and I was too young to understand what the pastor was saying in church.

But now that I'm older, I can read the Bible for myself! My favorite story is when Jesus fed 5,000 people with only five loaves of bread and two fish. That's just amazing! I can't even imagine what that much food would look like. You can read that story in Matthew 14:13–21, but here's what some of it looks like in Yopno.

You know, every time a language gets a Bible, it's kind of like Jesus multiplying the fish and loaves of bread. One Bible can reach many people who speak that language, and people who decide to believe in Jesus can multiply over and over again. That's one of the coolest miracles of all!

13Yesu uŋun Jon aŋakba kimakgit dakon gen bin nandaŋek iyɨ gin bot kinda abidaŋek mɨktɨm amɨni minikon kigɨt. Kiŋakwan miŋat amɨn kabɨ madep

Yesu uŋudon kisak yaŋ nandaŋek kokupni yopmaŋ yopmaŋ aŋek pakbɨ ɨdap ɨleŋɨ naŋ yol aŋkɨwit. 14 Aŋakwa bot uŋun paŋkɨ ɨleŋɨkon agakw

FUN FACTS:

The cassowary is a really big bird found on Papua New Guinea and its surrounding islands. It's related to the emu and ostrich, and just like them, it can't fly. It's also the third tallest and second heaviest bird in the world.

The Island of New Guinea was named after the African country with the same name.

Papua New Guinea is one of the least explored areas in the world, and people believe that there are many animals and plants still waiting to be discovered!

← cassowary

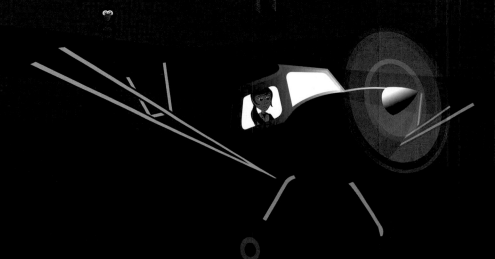

Papua New Guinea

Flag of Papua New Guinea

Yopno

It's really hard to travel around Papua New Guinea. Most people have to hike long distances, and if they want to get from one major place to another, they have to go by airplane or boat.

zᶻᶻ

Zinza

(Zeen-zah)

Moses

I'm Moses, and I live in Tanzania. Kate's been telling me about your trip and all that you've learned so far! It sounds like you've visited a lot of different countries, and now you're almost done with your trip around the world.

But before you go, I want to tell you about my people. Some of us are farmers. We grow different types of food like tropical fruits, beans, and plantains. Have you ever heard of plantains? They look kind of like a banana, but they aren't sweet. Usually people cook them before they eat them.

← goat

Anyways, we don't just grow food. Some of us are fishermen. Other people raise animals, like cows, sheep, and goats. My dad works with animals, and he lets me help him. My favorite time of year is when all the baby animals are born!

As we work, we usually speak our own language. It's called Zinza. But when we talk to people from different communities, we use Swahili.

That's one of the languages that most people in Tanzania speak. Swahili is also the language that is used in churches. When the pastor preaches, he reads from the Bible in Swahili. We all know how to talk about everyday things in Swahili, but we don't know the language well enough to talk about God and Heaven. Things like that are much easier to understand in our own language.

There are parts of the Bible that were translated into Zinza almost 100 years ago, but the alphabet they used is hard for us to read. So now people are working on making a new alphabet that is easier for us to understand. And they're starting to translate the Bible too!

↑ COW

93

We already have a little book called the *Way of Salvation* that has been published. This little book helps us understand the story of Jesus's death on the cross, and tells us how we can believe in Him. The book of Genesis has also been translated, so we know how God made the world and all the stories from the beginning up to when God's people—the Israelites—lived in Egypt.

Reading those stories makes me really excited to keep reading the Bible! I can't wait until more and more stories are translated into Zinza. Then I will be able to read them in my own language, not just listen to them in Swahili. And the more stories that are in Zinza, the more people will hear about Jesus. I want to tell everyone I know about the God of the Bible, so that they can know Him too!

FUN FACTS:

- Tanzania is the biggest country in East Africa. It includes three islands—Zanzibar, Pemba, and Mafia.

- Time in Tanzania is counted differently than the rest of the world. The work day starts at 6:00 a.m., which they call the first hour of the day. So if they said something starts at eight, they actually mean 2:00 p.m.

- The coconut crab is the world's biggest crab. It can be found on Chumbe Island of Zanzibar. This crab can weigh up to nine pounds and grow to be three feet long from leg to leg!

coconut crab

Tanzania has one of the only
tree-climbing lion populations
in the world, living in the Lake Manyara
National Park. The country also has the largest
concentration of wild animals for every square
kilometer (there are 1.6 kilometers in a mile).
There are more than four million wild animals
that live there!

tree-climbing lion

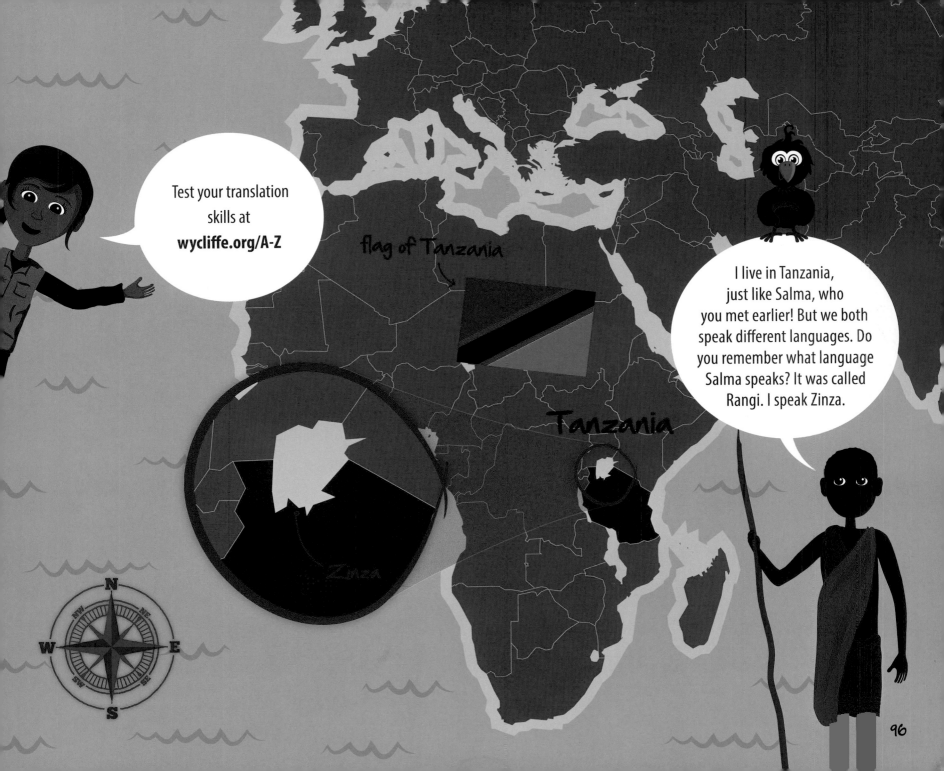

Well kids, we've been to 20 countries, met new friends who speak different languages, and learned a lot about Bible translation. That's a lot of traveling and learning!

I love visiting new places and meeting kids who are different than me. But even if we speak different languages or come from different cultures, there's one thing that's the same for all of us. Can you guess what that is?

It's that God loves us and speaks all of our languages—every single one in the whole world! And like we learned at the beginning of our trip, there are almost 7,000 langauges. That's a lot of languages to speak, but God made them all!

Next time you read your Bible, think of how blessed you are! It's easy to forget that the Bible hasn't always been in English, but it's true. And just like it had to be translated into English for us, it still has to be translated into other languages too.

Wycliffe

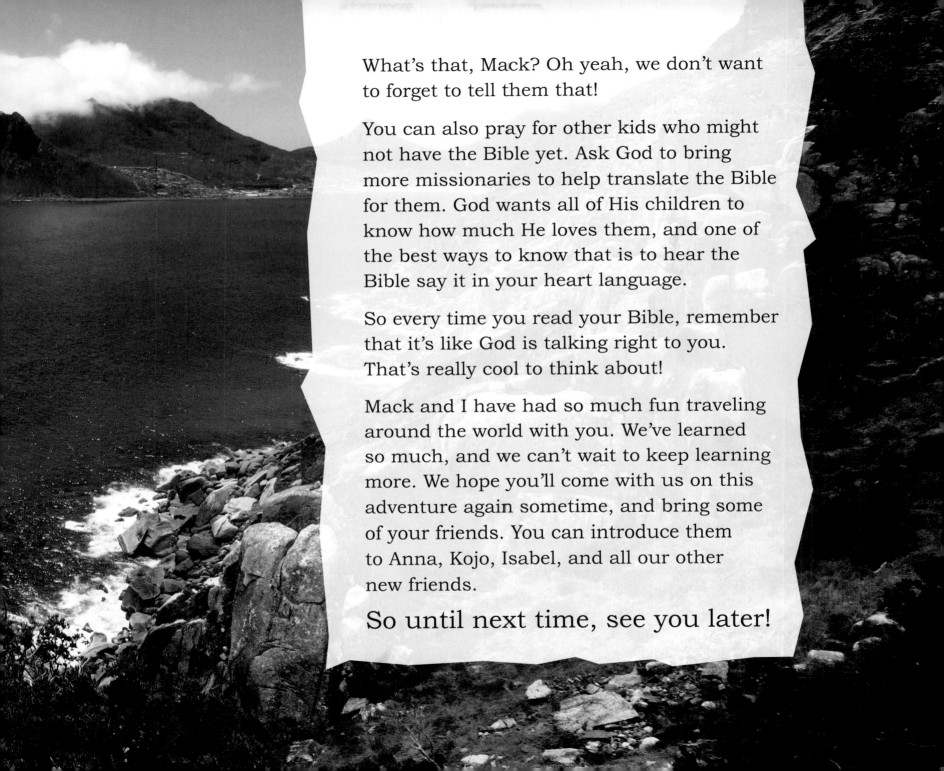

What's that, Mack? Oh yeah, we don't want to forget to tell them that!

You can also pray for other kids who might not have the Bible yet. Ask God to bring more missionaries to help translate the Bible for them. God wants all of His children to know how much He loves them, and one of the best ways to know that is to hear the Bible say it in your heart language.

So every time you read your Bible, remember that it's like God is talking right to you. That's really cool to think about!

Mack and I have had so much fun traveling around the world with you. We've learned so much, and we can't wait to keep learning more. We hope you'll come with us on this adventure again sometime, and bring some of your friends. You can introduce them to Anna, Kojo, Isabel, and all our other new friends.

So until next time, see you later!

WORLD
MAP

Special Thanks...

Many people have played significant roles in the ideation of this book. Some of those people include Annette Amdahl, Kristie Frieze, Jared Honaker, Christina Kapp, Dorothea Lander, Jan Mayer, Dustin Moody, Matt Petersen, Ken Pratt, Carol Signorino, Marilyn West, and Kathy Zoetewey. Thank you for all you did to help contribute to this book and bring it to life.

We'd also like to especially thank our "test group" who gave us their thoughts about Kate and Mack's adventure and how to make this a book that kids their age would love. Thanks to Emily Butler, Kenny Decker, Emily Guyadeen, Ariel Mullis, Nuriya Mullis, Alena Sandifer, Leslie Sandifer, Glenn (GT) Thomas, Rileigh Weiss, and Anna Colletto for your creative thoughts and ideas!

And to our new missionary kids who helped in later phases of this book, we're grateful for your thoughts and ideas as well! Thanks to Chloe Eiswald, Brianna Miller, Jake Miller, Karissa Miller, Adriel Near, Naaryah Near, Naomi Near, Obadiah Near, Jonathan Pirolo, Naomi Pirolo, Austin Romito, Bailey Romito, and Savannah Weiss.

Lastly, we'd like to thank Ann Marie Josten (researcher), June Hathersmith (author), and Alice Roder (artist) for the previous editions of A to Z books, which helped tell many readers about Bibleless people groups of the world who were waiting to receive God's Word in the language they understand best.

About Wycliffe

Wycliffe Bible Translators seeks to make the Bible accessible to all people in the language they understand best. Today more than one-fourth of the world's languages still have no Scripture.

To learn more about Wycliffe's work around the world, visit wycliffe.org.

About the designer

Ben Rupp is an artist proficient in painting, graphic design, photography, and bookbinding. He and his fiancée, Hannah, enjoy using their artistic talents to make the world a more beautiful place. Ben grew up in Florida and works as a graphic designer in Orlando.

About the author

Melissa Paredes was a Wycliffe missionary kid, so the opportunity to tell the story of kids, their languages, and their need for God's Word is a special privilege. She and her husband, Sam, enjoy working with kids and helping them learn more about the world. Melissa grew up in the Philippines, but now works as a writer in Orlando, Florida.

Melissa

Ben

The fun doesn't have to stop just because you've finished the book!

Come help Anna and the Arop people find a new village home. Or find out what your name would be if you lived in Ghana, like Kojo! You can even test your puzzle-solving skills with Sudoku from China.

Visit
for games, activities, recipes, and more!

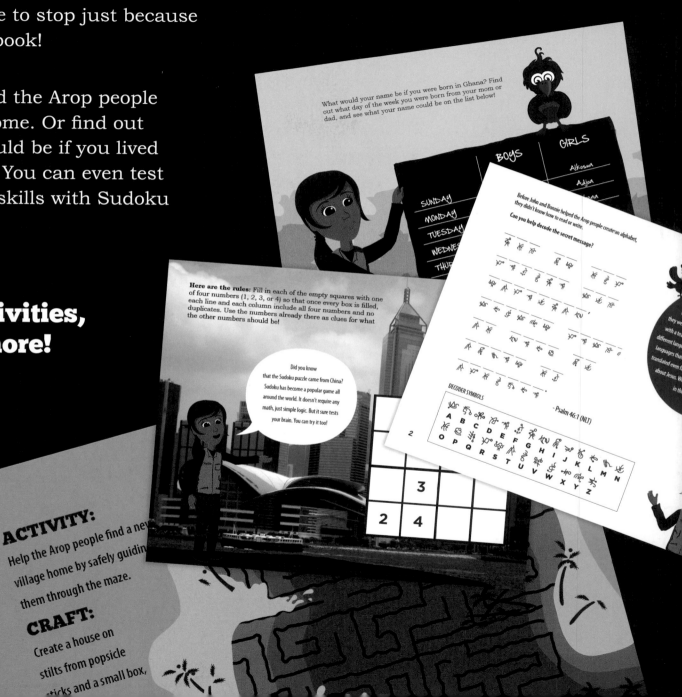

After this I looked, and there before me was a great multitude that no one could count, from every nation, tribe, people and language, standing before the throne and before the Lamb. They were wearing white robes and were holding palm branches in their hands. And they cried out in a loud voice:

"Salvation belongs to our God,
who sits on the throne,
and to the Lamb."

–Revelation 7:9-10 (NLT)